Surviving Your Blessings

OTHER BOOKS AND AUDIO BOOKS
BY LYNN C. JAYNES:

Fast Track to Heaven

Heaven Bound

Surviving Your Blessings

Learning to Laugh
in the Face of Life's Storms

lynn c. jaynes

Covenant Communications, Inc.

To my granddaughters, present and future, who will someday, at times, find themselves a little pockmarked.

Cover image by Rebecca Stuhff. For information email rstuhff@gmail.com © Covenant Communications, Inc.

Cover design copyrighted 2010 by Covenant Communications, Inc.

Published by Covenant Communications, Inc.
American Fork, Utah

Printed in Canada
First Printing: March 2010

16 15 14 13 12 11 10   10 9 8 7 6 5 4 3 2 1

ISBN 978-1-59811-918-3

Contents

CHAPTER 1

It's Not About You

A child once taught me a great lesson. I went to the state basketball tournament one year after following the local high school team through a turbulent season. After a particularly exciting, nail-biting state tournament basketball game (and we were darn lucky to have qualified for the tournament to begin with), I immediately called my young friend to share my excitement. "Hey, we won! We won! It was great! We won!"

"We did? We won?" His voice reflected all the excitement that I felt.

"Yeah, we won the basketball game! It was so great!" I was riding a high and couldn't seem to stop yelling.

"Oh, boy! We won!" Pause. And then hesitantly he asked, "Um, *what* did we win?" Even though he was only five years old, he had been to a couple of games with me that season, so I was surprised he wasn't grasping the concept.

"We won the basketball game. We won the tournament game." I realized then that he wasn't understanding the concept of tournament so I tried to keep my explanation simple. "Filer won the basketball game!"

"Oh, good!" He was trying to be as excited as I was but, bless his heart, he paused again. "Um, are we Filer . . . ?"

The spontaneity of the moment was beginning to wane as he belabored the point. "Yeah, we're Filer."

And then he fired right back up again. "Oh, good. We won! We won!" And he gave me all the exuberance he could muster, just because he wanted to share the excitement with me—or for me—he wasn't sure.

It reminded me of Alma at the Waters of Mormon when he complimented the people and described them as "willing to bear one another's burdens, that they may be light; yea, and are willing to mourn with those that mourn; yea, and comfort those that stand in need of comfort, and to stand as witnesses of God at all times and in all things, and in all places" (Mosiah 18:8–9). My little friend had gone one step further—he was willing to rejoice with those who were rejoicing, yell excitedly with those who were yelling excitedly, be animated with those who were being animated, cheer and celebrate with those who were cheering and celebrating.

It occurs to me that as members of a community or congregation, we're pretty good at attending funerals—mourning with those who mourn. We're probably average when it comes to rejoicing with those who are rejoicing, like at birthday parties, baby blessings, and baptisms. But where we really fall short is appreciating the excitement of another's achievement.

I remember several years ago a stake Relief Society put together some "achievement" tables where women were asked to share something they had accomplished through the year—whatever it was. There were no pre-qualifiers (like music, art—you know, the usuals); whatever anyone had achieved was fair game. The tables were on display in the cultural hall after the general Relief Society meeting held in the fall. I thoroughly enjoyed the display and was rejuvenated by all the creativity it represented. There were some really astounding achievements displayed along with fairly common ones—quilts, poetry, mending, family history collections, musical instruments, embroidery, cross-stitched items, jams and jellies, baked goods, painted items, tatted doilies, handmade jewelry, scrapbooks, photography, art—and several dozen other unique contributions. It was awesome.

The following year, however, there was no display. When I questioned why, I was told that not everyone was rejuvenated and uplifted by the display of skills. Someone had complained that the tables of achievement had left some sisters feeling untalented and unskilled, as though they had nothing valuable to contribute themselves. I was dumbfounded. I couldn't believe that wonderful, worthy display had been turned into something defeating. I wanted to smack someone. I wanted to put my hands on the sides of those sisters' faces, squeeze their little blush-covered cheeks, and say, "Honey, this is not about you. This is not a display about your insecurities. This is not a statement about who you *aren't*. This is about creativity. God creates, you know. It's a good thing."

Mourning with those who mourn is a good thing. Comforting those in need of comfort is also essential to being a disciple. But it seems incomplete, to me, if we don't also rejoice with those who are rejoicing and cheer for those who are excelling. A child inherently seems to know this. It's us adults who tend to forget. Mourning, comforting, rejoicing, and cheering— it's all part of standing as witnesses to each other's lives.

CHAPTER 2

Teaching the Teacher

I just want you all to know straight out that I am not related to any Youngs, Smiths, Kimballs, Monsons, Bensons, Packers, or Hinckleys. I do not have any direct ancestors who were mission presidents or stake presidents (that I know of). I do not have even thirdhand experiences or conversations with General Authorities to relate. I did not have an ancestor who pulled a handcart, received frostbite, or was buried on the plains. My ancestor who came across the plains in a wagon got in an argument with another wagon driver and, as the story goes, a few fists were thrown (you'll not likely hear about *that* one at general conference). I don't even know someone who knows someone who knows someone who might have known a prophet. I do, however, come from a long line of Primary, Sunday School, seminary, and Young Women teachers. It's my heritage.

I taught Sunbeams first—three little boys and four little girls.

A word about Sunbeams. One day I asked the Sunbeams what was new this week, and little Denny Peters said his daddy got a new pickup. I said, "Wow, that's really great; what color is it?" And he said, "Green and red and orange and brown." Come to find out, his dad had "acquired" a new irrigating pickup, which was a clunker from the get-go, was pieced together with fenders and a bed from who knows how many different vehicles, and probably had holes in the floorboards to boot. But that little Sunbeam was just as proud of it as if it had been a three-quarter-ton Power Stroke with all the trimmings.

I had such dreams for my little Sunbeam class. I was going to excite them about the gospel, set their minds firmly on serving missions, and help them awaken the kindness and charity that was just waiting to wiggle its way out of them. I taught two whole weeks before reality slapped me in the face and I faced the awful truth—*if* they were just sitting with their bottoms on their chairs, feet on the floor, and dresses in their laps (instead of over their heads) by the end of the year, then I would have accomplished the impossible. I cried every Sunday for the next two months.

I should have bucked up. Had I known that Sunbeams were a piece of cake compared to, well, practically everybody else, I'd have surely been a happy camper. I think it was the Mia Maids who really knocked the wind out of me. Mia Maids are ornery (don't you know) just because they can be. Their parents know nothing, their leaders know nothing, and me, as their teacher, not only knew nothing but was annoying as heck. I nagged them to participate in this or that activity and was always met with the same scowl, assuring me of my eternal lameness. I refused to be the "best friend" type of teacher—the one who would stay up late giggling and rehashing boy problems, talking about romantic loves, and reliving my own youth. They deserved better. I tried to give them discipline, and maybe I overdid it. I cried many activity nights. Whatever I tried didn't seem to work. The problem wasn't really them, it was me.

Then there were the Cub Scouts to teach, the Laurels, Relief Society sisters, and various ages of Sunday School children. I didn't hit full stride until the seminary years. By that time, I think I'd been teaching on and off for roughly twenty years. In seminary I taught the high school freshmen, mostly. We danced Virginia reels to learn about crossing the plains. We reenacted the Passover. We vied to be King instead of Scum during scripture chases. We tried to identify with Isaiah's approach to spiritual things. We made movies and had charades. Best of all, we began to really understand scripture together. We learned to testify.

They were the ones who finally taught me how to teach. They taught me that a class can be active but still worshipful, noisy but still reverent (yes, being reverent doesn't mean your tongue is cut out). And then, it was when I finally learned to be quiet that I learned about real teaching. When I was comfortable with my knowledge of the gospel, when I read and prepared but then didn't fret over the presentation, when I learned a few tricks that worked every single time, I finally had the confidence to shut up and let the kids actually learn by participating. And participating more, and participating until they were discovering things for themselves and learning how to learn. It was exciting.

Teaching was a long journey. A very long journey. I started out as a full-fledged greenie, prepared all the wrong ways, tried all the wrong things. I wanted to quit several times. I trudged through a few rough deserts of my own, I guess, felt cold and disheartened more than once, and was grateful for the rescue parties that sometimes showed up. But eventually it became easier. Eventually things started to roll. Eventually I hit my stride.

And then, all of a sudden, the journey was over. It took me twenty-four years, lots of preparation, and lots of prayer to get just pretty fair at it. Then they released me. Unyoked me. Unhitched me. Haven't had a teaching calling since. Nada. I'd like to put my little dress up over my little head, sit in my little corner, and have a good little cry. But I won't. That would tarnish the heritage I must hand down to my children— who aren't related to any Youngs, Smiths, Kimballs, Monsons, Bensons, Packers, or Hinckleys either, and did not have an ancestor who pulled a handcart, received frostbite, or was buried on the plains.

CHAPTER 3

Lava and Granite

Lava rock is ugly. It's black and doesn't shine. It is pockmarked. Millions of years ago when it came out of the ground in southern Idaho, it formed some scoria lava tubes that are kind of cool, except for the fact that they are black, dull, pockmarked and . . . that's it. Then the lava tubes, which could have been interesting formations, just collapsed—or most of them did, anyway. Some sources say Idaho's lava even ended up as far away as Chicago. (I just thought I'd throw that in.)

You can't polish lava rock because the force breaks it apart. Any old thing breaks it apart. It's so pockmarked that when water gets inside and freezes, the expansion of the water breaks the lava rock. That's why we have no lava peaks. It's no match for the wind and storms. It's not good for decorative rock for your fireplace, either, because too many spiders can hide in it and you can't dust it. It isn't fashioned to make anything useful; if early Americans ever used it for bowls, utensils, buttons, or anything else, we have no evidence of it because the dumb stuff broke apart (and left them toothless and naked, no doubt). Only lizards and snakes like lava rock (I'm guessing it scratches their bellies), and that's really not much of a recommendation in my opinion.

Granite is everything lava is not. It's solid. It polishes beautifully. It weathers slowly and creates majestic, craggy peaks. The central Idaho wilderness is renowned for its breathtaking granite peaks (breathtaking in part because by the time you backpack to the top of them, you are short on oxygen and literally out of breath). It comes in different colors—high-shine black, pinks, grays, whites, even yellow. It's useful; early Americans applied force to granite and formed pestles and bowls to grind grains. Granite is beautiful and highly sought after. Everybody likes granite. It's even become a symbol of prestige and wealth when used in kitchen countertops, bathtubs, and such.

Two rocks—so different, but interestingly enough, they are the same thing. Lava rock was magma that cooled above ground very rapidly. This made it brittle. Above ground it was exposed to gas bubbles, ash, other impurities, and air, which created the pockmark effect. On the other hand, granite was magma that cooled slowly underground with time and pressure, then more time and more pressure, and still more time and still more pressure. You can't rush solid granite. It must be excruciatingly hot for an unfathomably long time. Heavenly Father did not take shortcuts creating something that deep, magnificent, and strong. Anything less, of course, any shortcut or mitigation of the process at all, would have created long-term problems and fatal flaws like brittleness and pockmarks. There was just no other way.

Lava and granite—two rocks of the same substance, developed under different circumstances. Yet, remember this—at any given time *one was only a meltdown away from becoming the other.*

It seems to me that many women consider themselves to be like lava—dull and uninteresting, pockmarked with impurities and weaknesses. Their children don't spout scriptures, sometimes call each other names, and are occasionally (can it be?) selfish. They'll die of embarrassment if someone pulls out their washer or dryer knowing that lint, dirt, powdered Tide, and the occasional stray sock are going to have to be chipped off the floor with a pancake turner. They're tired after every workday and want so much to collapse in front of the TV or read a mind-numbing novel instead of engaging in more worthy pursuits because they just don't have the energy for one more goal. The list of demands on their time grows excruciatingly long, and personal pursuits seem to be unfathomably distant.

What's more, these sisters often presume that the majority of the *other sisters* in the Church are of the granite variety. You know them; they're highly polished, solid, so talented and useful—the kind who sing in choirs dressed in three-piece suits with jewelry that didn't come from an eleven-year-old on Mother's Day. Other granite sisters direct ward roadshows, create programs for Relief Society birthday dinners, are 100 percent visiting teachers, actually know what's in their food storage, and have children who perpetually seem to be either on missions or being married in the temple, receiving Eagle Scout awards or Young Womanhood Recognition awards, and receiving scholarships. Granite women can be as intimidating sometimes as the granite peaks themselves, especially to those feeling like the brittle lava-bed kind.

I'm not a geologist, but there is a rock-like correlation to life. The day I taught Sunbeams and realized it would be a struggle just to keep their dresses in their laps, I was having a lava moment. Lava moments are times when I have felt barren and unproductive, rude, critical, discouraged, or inadequate. I've had my share. But given time, these are usually followed by some granite moments—times when I was kind, creative, prepared, or gracious, or when I shined in some other way. Sometimes opportunities presented themselves and broke me apart, which allowed later opportunities to make of me something quite useful.

I think everyone has lava moments and granite moments. I give you Nephi as an example. Here is one of his lava moments: "O wretched man that I am! Yea, my heart sorroweth because of my flesh; my soul grieveth because of mine iniquities. I am encompassed about, because of the temptations and the sins which do so easily beset me." And then the meltdown begins. Feeling somewhat pockmarked, Nephi, almost within the same breath, experiences intense heat and pressure and ultimately has a granite moment: "O Lord, I have trusted in thee, and I will trust in thee forever. . . . I will lift up my voice unto thee; yea, I will cry unto thee, my God, the rock of my righteousness.

Behold, my voice shall forever ascend up unto thee, my rock and mine everlasting God" (2 Nephi 4:17–18, 34–35).

We have to consider the moment Moses parted the Red Sea as a solidly polished granite moment. However, when the Lord first called him to deliver Israel, he had his lava moments. "And Moses said unto God, Who am I, that I should go unto Pharaoh, and that I should bring forth the children of Israel out of Egypt? . . . And Moses said unto the LORD, O my Lord, I am not eloquent, neither heretofore, nor since thou hast spoken unto thy servant: but I am slow of speech, and of a slow tongue" (Exodus 3:11, 4:10).

Joseph Smith certainly had a granite moment when he received the First Vision, but he later had several lava moments when he doubted his abilities and felt unpolished.

> During the space of time which intervened between the time I had the vision and the year eighteen hundred and twenty-three . . . I was left to all kinds of temptations; and, mingling with all kinds of society, I frequently fell into many foolish errors, and displayed the weakness of youth, and the foibles of human nature; which, I am sorry to say, led me into divers temptations, offensive in the sight of God. . . .
>
> In consequence of these things, I often felt condemned for my weakness and imperfections. (Joseph Smith—History 1:28–29)

I think if anyone were to ask me on any given day whether I was having a granite or lava day, I would reply simply, "Uh-huh." In other words, I'm probably having both—just give me a minute. And I'm okay with that. Granite has a purpose. So does lava.

In addition, I'm not particularly concerned whether other sisters consider themselves lava or granite at any given moment. If you're having a granite day, then good for you. If you're having a lava day, well, go have a good cry and remember it doesn't mean every day will be lava. A lot of lava things happen that are no one's fault. It's part of the process we're here to experience. Granite, as you recall, takes heat, time, and pressure. Lots of it. Just remember that at any moment, you *are only one meltdown away from becoming the other.*

CHAPTER 4

Laws Irrevocably Decreed

There are plenty of mathematical and scientific laws regarding our universe that scholars have "discovered" and thankfully have explained to the rest of us. I am just a humble, modest, unpretentious, unassuming (albeit heavy on the adjectives) *genius* myself. I seek no credit or fame (although some obscenely large study grant would be nice), but I think it's time I came forward and thoroughly impressed the world with my discovery of universal laws as well. Pay attention.

An irrevocable law: If you pull that string hanging from your sleeve, you *will* lose a button. If you pull that string hanging from your hem, you *will* lose a button. If you pull that string from the tag at the back of your neck, you *will* lose a button.

An irrevocable law: If you attend the Family Relations class during Sunday School, you'll soon find that:

a. Your relationships are not half as messed up as some in the ward.

b. Men and women don't communicate the same; men talk too slow. I was informed that this is because women talk too fast. Although it really shouldn't have to be said, the *reason* women talk too fast is because men are only going to listen for thirty seconds anyway, *so we have to make that thirty seconds count.*

c. No matter what family relations experience a classmate has to share, another classmate can top it.

d. I can only keep quiet in the Family Relations class for just sooooo long before I erupt. This could be why people avoid me.

16

All right, I haven't conducted enough research to actually publish my findings in a trade publication, but I'm pretty sure they're correct. No, not *pretty sure*. I am right; that's all there is to it. Which brings me to another point: I was taught in that same Family Relations class that it doesn't matter who's right. Well, that's just clap-trap. I know God cares about being right. Therefore, I am going to pronounce another irrevocable law—I cannot keep my mouth shut in the Family Relations class. (You thought I was going to say I'm always right, didn't you? Silly you—it goes without saying.) They just need *too much direction* in that class and, really girls, it's wearing me out.

One guy I've heard about who found an irrevocable law was Archimedes (287–212 BC), sometimes referred to as the Father of Buoyancy. Before that, he was known as an eccentric nerd in Syracuse. Apparently, he was one of those children who would rather draw mathematical figures in the dirt than take a bath or play games. He even carried around a box of sand for his proofs and theorems (the equivalent of a laptop).

Archimedes impressed King Hiero when King Hiero had a very large ship that had been built before anyone figured out how to launch it. Several men put their heads together to try to figure out how to launch this ship, but their combined strength and ingenuity were not equal to the task. Archimedes studied the problem, then built a compound machine based on a system of levers and pulleys. When he was ready, he had the men fully load the ship with cargo and crew. He then put a rope that would operate his contraption into Hiero's hand and told him to pull. That one man (the king) with that one rope successfully launched the ship.

Archimedes also used his ingenuity to help his countrymen at war. After King Hiero died, Hieronymus took the throne and joined with Carthage in fighting against Rome. A Roman leader soon blocked the harbor with ships and led his army to the gates of Syracuse. Archimedes devised cranes similar to the ones used today and used grappling hooks to snag the enemy ships. He raised the ships into the air and then dropped them, smashing them into the water. He also swung some of the ships over the city walls and lowered the ships and crew to the waiting Syracusians.

Now back to being the Father of Buoyancy—Archimedes is probably best known for an incident involving King Heiro's crown. As the story goes, the king gave a certain amount of gold to a craftsman to fashion a fine crown. After the crown was made, a rumor flew through the town claiming the craftsman had fraudulently substituted some silver in place of some of the gold, thereby devaluing the crown. Archimedes was given the task of determining whether the crown was pure gold or not.

As Archimedes considered the problem, he happened to go to the baths. When he lowered himself into the bathing pool he noticed that the amount of water that overflowed the pool's lip was equal to the volume of his body that was immersed. Apparently, this was the answer he sought. He was so excited that he leapt from the pool and ran home naked shouting, "Eureka! Eureka!" (Greek for "I have found it.")

What Archimedes found was the principle of buoyancy. Simply stated, it is this: an object immersed in a fluid displaces the same volume of fluid as the volume of the object. Thus, it was possible to determine the precise volume of the crown by immersing it in water, then fashion a piece of gold that would equal that volume. This fashioned piece of gold could then be compared to the block of gold the craftsman had been given with which to fashion the crown. Was it larger or was it smaller? The two blocks of gold were then placed in a balance and it was discovered they did not have equal mass. Thus it was determined that the craftsman had substituted silver for gold and in the face of this evidence, the craftsman confessed his crime.

The principle of buoyancy seems to be an irrevocable law. There are also laws that govern spiritual matters:

- "I, the Lord, am bound when ye do what I say; but when ye do not what I say, ye have no promise" (D&C 82:10).

- "Therefore, I give unto you this commandment, that ye bind yourselves by this covenant, and it shall be done according to the laws of the Lord" (D&C 82:15).

- "There is a law, irrevocably decreed in heaven before the foundations of this world, upon which all blessings are predicated—And when we obtain any blessing from God, it is by obedience to that law upon which it is predicated" (D&C 130:20–21).

The law works both ways—when I keep the law, I receive the blessing, but when I do not keep the law, then I receive no blessing. I prefer to focus on the positive. If I go to that Family Relations class, bite my tongue, and cease to find fault with everyone else's relationships (and I'm *working on that one*), then I will be humble enough to improve my own relationships. Or maybe the *family* would be blessed enough to recognize that I'm right (but I won't hold my breath).

Wait a minute—why did I say that? Am I back in the very same hole I started out in? Yes, I think I am. I'm sure I had a good thought here when I began—something about irrevocable laws and the consequences of such. Something about obedience. I was sure this was going to be really profound, an epiphany, but now I've lost it. The only irrevocable law I seem to have proven is that I dig the hole, try to climb out of the hole, and then find myself at the very bottom of the hole all over again, and I'm still surprised by the process.

There ought to be a support group for this.

CHAPTER 5

Tsunamis

I did a little research on tsunamis, and this is what I found. Tsunamis are created in a variety of ways—earthquakes, volcanic eruptions, landslides, and asteroids striking Earth. Any major force that causes a major land shift has the potential to create a tsunami.

Tsunamis occur principally in the Pacific Ocean, which has the most active hotspots, but they have occurred in every ocean. Many have single wavelengths up to several hundred miles long and can travel at speeds of up to 450 miles per hour. Contrast this with a regular ocean wave caused by wind, which travels from a few miles per hour up to 60 miles per hour.

Many tsunamis have wave heights less than three feet high in deep ocean water and will pass unnoticed beneath ships at sea. The wave height increases with catastrophic results as the wave nears shallow shorelines. These waves can travel across the Pacific Ocean in less than one day. If a tsunami is generated fairly locally, then the wave can reach coastlines in just minutes.

A tsunami generally consists of a series of waves, referred to as the tsunami wave train. The amount of time between waves, known as the wave period, is generally only a few minutes, but at times the waves have been more than an hour apart. This deceptive and dangerous lull between waves can cause individuals to think the tsunami is past and go nearer the shoreline to begin assessing damages, only to be met with another tsunami wave.

Probably the most destructive tsunami ever recorded occurred following the eruption of the volcano Krakatoa in the East Indies on August 27, 1883. More than 36,000 people were killed as a result. Waves were recorded at 100 feet high with speeds between 350 and 450 miles per hour. Another disaster is believed to have occurred around AD 1500 when a 0.6-mile-wide asteroid struck the ocean southwest of New Zealand, creating multiple tsunamis that reached heights of more than 425 feet.

This is all quite fascinating in a morbid, dangerously exciting kind of way. I was awestruck when the tsunami hit Indonesia in 2004. I remember watching those newscasts in a horrified, fixed stare, unable to tear myself away from the incredible sights captured on camera. I was awestruck by the energy and power behind such a force. One report said the tsunami affected Earth's rotation by increasing the length of the day by 2.68 nanoseconds. It literally knocked the earth off its rocker!

I've never experienced a natural disaster—no hurricanes, no tornadoes, no volcanic eruptions, no earthquake of note. Even though I live in a moderate earthquake zone, apparently the lava bedrock under my part of the country absorbs shockwaves. So even though we've had a few recorded earthquake tremblers, I can't say I felt them much, and I certainly can't say that I suffered because of them.

I was in the Rexburg, Idaho, area with a group of 4-H kids when the Teton Dam broke, but at the first radio broadcast of that disaster, we loaded up in the vans and raced home before the floodwaters hit. I did participate in some of the cleanup, though. I went with a group of Church youth to the area some weeks later to help shovel muck and mud from the homes. I remember it quite clearly because I didn't know quite what I was up against and had innocently taken a bucket, some cleaning chemicals, and a few old rags with me. Imagine my surprise when the bus drove through that town with homes knocked off their foundations and basements literally filled with mud. Automobiles had been deposited into the middle of fields, along with piles of unidentifiable metal and debris. I was once again transfixed by the energy and power behind such a force.

The woman in Sugar City whose home I was assigned to help clean asked me as I was leaving that day if I would mind if she kept my rags. I must have looked a little askance that she would want my rags—her home was still at the shovel-the-mud-out stage, and we had used hammers to knock out sheetrock most of the day. What could she possibly want with my rags? Then she said, "My husband and I have been living at the college campus, and we don't have any washrags. I'd like to keep them to use as washrags." I wondered again about the power and force that had brought this woman, who, it seemed, was used to comfortable means to humbly ask if she could have just a few of my rags.

And so the forces of the earth rage and will continue until Christ comes again. But those are only the external upheavals. There will also be internal ones.

Elder Jeffrey R. Holland said:

The first words Jesus spoke in His majestic Sermon on the Mount were to the troubled, the discouraged and downhearted. "Blessed are the poor in spirit," He said, "for theirs is the kingdom of heaven." . . . I speak to those who are facing personal trials and family struggles, those who endure conflicts fought in the lonely foxholes of the heart, those trying to hold back floodwaters of despair that sometimes wash over us like a *tsunami of the soul.* ("Broken Things to Mend," *Ensign,* May 2006, 69; emphasis added)

That kind of tsunami I know. I don't want to exaggerate my difficult experiences—I'm sure yours have been just as difficult. When my family had a tsunami of the soul, my sister was talking with a friend who was going through a difficult time with his family as well. His comment to my sister was, "My problems are as big to me as yours are to you." At first I thought the guy was nuts. I thought he had no idea what he was saying. How could he begin to compare his "problem" with ours? It took me a while to understand what he was saying and to believe him. Now I have no doubt he experienced a tsunami as well.

I'm sure you know what I'm talking about—those experiences that literally wash over us and drag us rolling and tumbling through all kinds of dirt and debris, leaving us breathless and struggling for air. It doesn't really matter what caused it; it consumes our energy within its own. The force behind this kind of tsunami is no less devastating than that caused by an asteroid hitting the earth. The only question is whether we can hang on long enough to weather it through.

Well, enough of that. Let's not dwell on it. We can't stand transfixed forever at such scenes of devastation without at some point asking ourselves what we're going to do about it. Elder Holland continued:

> To you who feel your lives are broken . . . I offer the surest and sweetest remedy that I know. It is found in the clarion call the Savior of the world Himself gave. . . . He said to everyone, whatever their personal problems might be: "Come unto me, all ye that labour and are heavy laden, and I will give you rest. Take my yoke upon you, and learn of me; for I am meek and lowly in heart: and ye shall find rest unto your souls." (69)

One way to come unto Christ is to have hope and believe in His power. It's not difficult to believe in the power of destruction, because we see that. The question is can we also see the healing power and force of our Savior? Can we believe in that? There was hope, I think, in the woman who asked for my rags. She was discouraged, yes, but she also didn't see herself giving up. If she had given up, she never would have asked for my rags.

Elder Joseph B. Wirthlin said:

> Many today feel troubled and distressed; many feel that, at any moment, the ships of their lives could capsize or

sink. It is to you who are looking for a safe harbor that I wish to speak today, you whose hearts are breaking, you who are worried or afraid, you who bear grief or the burdens of sin, you who feel no one is listening to your cries, you whose hearts are pleading, "Master, carest thou not that I perish?" To you I offer a few words of comfort and of counsel.

Be assured that there is a safe harbor. . . . Your Heavenly Father—who knows when even a sparrow falls—knows of your heartache and suffering. He loves you and wants the best for you. . . . While He allows all of us to make choices that may not always be for our own or even others' well-being, and while He does not always intervene in the course of events, He has promised the faithful peace even in their trials and tribulations. ("Finding a Safe Harbor," *Ensign,* May 2000, 59)

This offers me hope. Just having someone be my strong captain and assure me that there is a safe harbor ahead brings me hope. I can hang on to that.

Second, we should change anything we have the power to change. In other words, start shoveling the mud. The woman in the Teton flood was working on salvaging her home and emptying out the food storage she had so obediently gathered. She worked right alongside me. She couldn't change the destruction that had descended upon her home with such fury, but there were things she could do to improve her situation. Likewise, you may not be able to change a loved one, or you may find yourself in a circumstance beyond your control. Nevertheless, there are things you can change. You can change the depth of your devotions, the consistency of your prayers, and the focus of your forgiveness, for example. You can change.

Third, we should strive to take upon ourselves the identity of Jesus Christ, whose covenant people we are. This begins with the covenants of baptism and partaking of the sacrament. It also involves participating in temple endowments, which provide us:

- "The power of enlightenment, of testimony, and of understanding" (David B. Haight, "Temples and Work Therein," *Ensign*, Nov. 1990, 61).

- Power to "thwart the forces of evil" (Ezra Taft Benson, *Teachings of Ezra Taft Benson* [Salt Lake City: Bookcraft, 1988], 256).

- "Power which enables us to use our gifts and capabilities with greater intelligence and increased effectiveness" (David B. Haight, "Come to the House of the Lord," *Ensign*, May 1992, 15).

- "Power to overcome the sins of the world and 'stand in holy places' (D&C 45:32)" (Glenn L. Pace, "Spiritual Revival," *Ensign*, Nov. 1992, 12).

- "Greater powers that [we] might be better qualified to teach" (Joseph Fielding Smith, *Doctrines of Salvation*, comp. Bruce R. McConkie, 3 vols. [Salt Lake City: Deseret News Press, 1954–56], 2:242).

- "Power with which to strengthen [our] earthly families" (Theodore M. Burton, "Salvation for the Dead—A Missionary Activity," *Ensign*, May 1975, 71).

- "The promised personal revelation that may bless [our] life with power, knowledge, light, beauty, and truth from on high" (Haight, "Come to the House of the Lord," 16).

When I take upon myself His identity, I become better equipped to make those changes that are within my power to change.

If you are experiencing a tsunami of the soul and feel a bit broken, I could bring you a casserole; I could even offer to take care of your ironing. But the best thing I can do for you is remind you of the Savior's words, "Come unto me," and tell you in the sincerity of my heart, "I'm sorry you're hurting."

In Nazareth, the narrow road,
That tires the feet and steals the breath,
Passes the place where once abode
The Carpenter of Nazareth.

And up and down the dusty way
The village folk would often wend;
And on the bench, beside Him, lay
Their broken things for Him to mend.

The maiden with the doll she broke,
The woman with the broken chair,
The man with broken plough, or yoke,
Said, "Can you mend it, Carpenter?"

And each received the thing he sought,
In yoke, or plough, or chair, or doll;
The broken thing which each had brought
Returned again a perfect whole.

So, up the hill the long years through,
With heavy step and wistful eye,
The burdened souls their way pursue,
Uttering each the plaintive cry:

"O Carpenter of Nazareth,
This heart, that's broken past repair,
This life, that's shattered nigh to death,
Oh, can You mend them, Carpenter?"

And by His kind and ready hand,
His own sweet life is woven through
Our broken lives, until they stand
A New Creation—"all things new."

"The shattered [substance] of [the] heart,
Desire, ambition, hope, and faith,
Mould Thou into the perfect part,
O, Carpenter of Nazareth!"

(George Blair, "The Carpenter of Nazareth," as quoted in Holland, "Broken Things to Mend," 71)

Sisters, if a tsunami of the soul is washing over you, you just hang in there. Its force will fade. And all of that tumbling and rolling will intensify your faith, strengthen your resolve to lift others who also experience tsunamis, and polish your character. It will leave you breathless.

CHAPTER 6

The Way the Wind Blows

Many people wonder, "Where did we come from? Why are we here?" and, "Where are we going?" Great questions. Lots of times my thoughts don't go that deep. Mostly I wonder, "Why can't I quit chewing my fingernails?" and, "Why aren't I living on Cherry Creek with Margaret?"

My cousin Margaret and I were fast friends in our youth. Her family visited mine a few times a year, and I spent several happy summers visiting her home in Logan. We rode bikes all up and down the streets of Logan and swung on the rope swing over the canal, which was a few short thousand blocks from her home. We dreamed and spun tales and made plans for the future.

My favorite fantasy with Margaret was dreaming of growing up to live side by side on Cherry Creek. We decided we would homeschool our children and our husbands would probably commute to work. Secretly, I thought it would be better if the husbands *did* have to commute to work because then they would be out of the way and wouldn't mess up our plans. Margaret and I were going to go back to the pioneer lifestyle to cook over fires and make our own soap. We were going to haul water in buckets and chop wood and build our own cabins. We would raise our own beef, chickens, and milk cows, grow our own gardens, and occasionally send the kids out to catch fish and pick wild berries. We would be wonderful mothers, and our children would grow up working hard with only pure influences on them—not influenced by the lack of values portrayed on television and elsewhere. We would visit back and forth at

Christmastime and for birthdays—just like in the movie *Seven Brides for Seven Brothers*. And Cherry Creek would be home.

The truth of it is I don't even know where Cherry Creek is anymore. When I went to it the first time I thought, "This is it? This is all there is? What's so great about Cherry Creek?" And I remember the brambles on the forest floor as quite a hindrance, unlike the lodgepole-pine forests where I grew up camping. I think we chose Cherry Creek because it was the mountain place Margaret had grown up with and had fallen in love with, and then she was insistent. I gave her that point. After all, woods are woods, and one creek is as good as the next. It was a great fantasy. They were great summer vacations with Margaret.

But I'm not living on Cherry Creek today, and neither is Margaret. Margaret and I even have trouble remembering each others' married names and the names of each others' children. I'll bet I can count on two hands the number of times we've seen each other since we got out of high school. Pity, that. I wonder sometimes if we have any of the same dreams left.

Where did I come from? Not Cherry Creek. Why am I here? Apparently not to be living a pioneer lifestyle with Margaret on Cherry Creek. Where am I going? Not sure, but if I get there I hope someone tells me when I've arrived. These sound more like questions we should ask of the wind.

Who has seen the wind?
Neither I nor you:
But when the leaves hang trembling
The wind is passing thro'.

Who has seen the wind?
Neither you nor I:
But when the trees bow down their heads
The wind is passing by.

(Christina Rossetti, "Who Has Seen the Wind?")

I know a whole lot more about wind than I do about Cherry Creek. Californians who move to southern Idaho are always disappointed to find they have to walk to their cars at a thirty-five degree angle. Visitors to the Gem State, amusingly enough, expect to find precious "gems" (and we're not going to get into a lengthy discussion over the definition of gems—so for now we'll just say our clean air, potato crops, trout streams, granite peaks, and lava fields are not on the table for discussion). What visitors to the Gem State get is wind, and I've wondered forever where it comes from, why it's here, and where it's going. So I did a little investigating.

At the risk of oversimplifying things, wind is moving air. When we see a hurricane, waves, or tornadoes, we are not seeing wind. Wind is invisible. We are seeing the effects of wind.

The sun is the basic reason we have weather. Most of the larger weather systems that move across our world develop because the sun's energy is not distributed equally over the globe. The sun shines most directly on low latitudes, which heats them to higher temperatures than polar regions. Another contributing factor is that Earth is tilted on an axis, with different parts of Earth being heated more, or heated less, depending on the time of year and axis tilt. Compounding this is the fact that land heats faster than water, creating temperature differences between oceans and continents. This unequal heating creates fluctuations in temperature and air pressure, winds, and ocean currents.

Earth is constantly trying to balance, or equalize, the variations in temperatures, so winds carry heat from the tropical regions toward the poles in a constant effort to reach a thermal balance. Where did wind come from? From heated air rising and cooler air rushing in to take its place. Why is it here? To equalize the earth's temperature. Where is it going? Sadly enough, to southern Idaho.

Where did I come from? Since even the wind knows where it came from, why it's here, and where it's going, then maybe I can figure out the same questions about me. Academically speaking,

I know where I came from. I can't remember it, but maybe that point isn't relevant. I've been taught, and I know that I have a Heavenly Father of my spirit. I am literally His child. I know this is true in my heart. I don't know how I know it's true, I just know that it is. It is just my Heavenly Father's gift to me. I wondered when I was growing up whether I had been born into the right family or not. Silly to wonder, maybe, but I certainly didn't feel that I fit the family. Sometimes when I was feeling low I'd wonder about the family that I dreamed was "supposed" to be mine. Was it the Williams family? They had no girls. Was it the Andreason family? They were welcoming enough but already had six. Was it Aunt Jean's family? They had no girls. Aunt Jean even asked once if she could adopt me (although I realize she may not have been serious). But even amidst my speculations, I did not have to speculate about a heavenly family. I knew I had a heavenly family, and I knew I fit there somewhere—even if it was just to dust the clouds.

Why am I here? There are things for me to learn in this life that I can learn in no other way. (While I'm going to ask for proof of this someday, for now I'll take it on faith.) A second reason is to obtain a physical body. This is vital. And further, I must be tried and tested. This really explains why Margaret and I aren't living on Cherry Creek. Apparently, we both needed some experiences that Cherry Creek couldn't give us. Speaking strictly for myself and not Margaret, I needed the experience of having a husband home on a daily basis. How would I have ever worked through the frustrations of marriage if my husband had constantly been gone? Who would have taught me not to yell so much? Who would have taught me not to take myself so seriously? Who would have told me to calm down? Not Margaret. I think I'd have plowed right over the top of her. I also needed to figure out where I fit in a community and in society in general. Apparently, I also needed the experiences and knowledge that I gained from living with the family of my childhood. I needed to figure out that I was okay, even if I didn't feel that I fit in. And let's face it; if I had homeschooled my children on Cherry Creek, then my children would stink at math.

Where am I going? That's the great part; it's up to me. I can return to live with Heavenly Father, or not. If I choose to return, then I have some work to do. "And now, my brethren, I would that . . . ye *come forth and bring fruit unto repentance.* Yea, I would that ye would come forth and harden not your hearts any longer; . . . and therefore, if ye will repent and harden not your hearts, immediately shall the great plan of redemption be brought about unto you. For behold, *this life is the time for men to prepare to meet God; yea, behold the day of this life is the day for men to perform their labors*" (Alma 34:30–32; emphasis added). My life's work really has nothing to do with chopping wood, milking cows, and gathering berries. My life's work has nothing to do with being a secretary, a nurse, an accountant, an educator, or a herdsman. My life's work has nothing to do with laundry, balancing checkbooks, or clipping coupons. If I want to return to my Heavenly Father, then it's my job to learn humility, make my will secondary to the will of my Heavenly Father, and repent—the same life's work as yours. I could have done that on Cherry Creek, I think. Maybe.

After those summers with Margaret, I have since learned to chop wood anyway, milk a cow, pick berries, make butter and cheese, cook over a fire, and all those other things we dreamed about. I would have loved learning all of those things on Cherry Creek with Margaret, but it wasn't in the plan. The wind just didn't blow that way.

CHAPTER 7

Wide Enough and Deep Enough

I should introduce you to Ralph. Ralph is the ghost in my red 2000 Ford Taurus. I first met Ralph when he was feeling neglected and he decided to turn on the windshield wipers for attention. This was funny, except for the fact that I couldn't turn them off. He now does this periodically as the mood suits him. The wipers just run until Ralph gets tired of the game; then he turns them off. There I'll be, humming down the road five miles an hour below the speed limit, tuning the radio to classic rock or golden oldies music, watching the hay fields and the progress of new subdivisions, and all of a sudden, Ralph will turn on the wipers and smear grasshoppers, bumble bees, gnats, and mosquitoes in an arc from one end of the windshield to the other. He thinks it's funny. He also thinks it's funny to not warm up the heater in midwinter until I arrive at my destination. And Ralph thinks it's a hoot to make the car smell sour for two days after every car wash. I accused him of *poor spirit hygiene* once and he denied it. But he's not fooling anybody; *that smell is just not natural.* Ralph is weird that way.

So anyway, Ralph and I got into this BIG discussion one day about whether I had a *life* or not (*like he did???* Surely you didn't miss the pun there, did you?). I argued that I did have a life, and I brought up the fact that I had a very interesting job at the police station in the detective division. As a consequence of that job, I had been to a crime scene, I had sat through court trials, I had prepared court documents, I had seen methamphetamine and marijuana, I had transcribed internal investigations up the yin-yang for minute things that no more needed an internal investigation than if someone had dropped a pencil on its lead instead of its eraser. *So don't tell me I don't have a life!* Ralph's reply was (and I quote), "Big whoop."

Ralph was insistent that to have a life, one has to continually learn and grow in strength of character, testimony, and humility. (He's philosophical.) To make my case that I had indeed done this, I told Ralph this story.

Several years ago (before I worked at the police station), I was reading through general conference talks, and somehow the testimonies borne at the end of each talk really caught my attention. They seemed pretty powerful. There was a depth or a feeling there that *I felt.* Most of them bore direct witness of the Atonement, and I decided that I wanted to know more about that feeling. The General Authorities *knew* something I didn't, and I wanted to know what that was. Now I don't pretend to have their calling as a special witness of Christ, but Brigham Young said, "There is no doubt, if a person lives according to the revelations given to God's people, he may have the Spirit of the Lord to signify to him his will, and to guide and to direct him in the discharge of his duties, in his temporal as well as his spiritual exercises. I am satisfied, however, that in this respect, *we live far beneath our privileges*" (*Discourses of Brigham Young,* sel. and arr. by John A. Widtsoe [Salt Lake City: Deseret Book, 1977], 32; emphasis added).

So I set out on a quest to figure out more of the Atonement than I had known before. I looked in the scriptures, I dug up old talks from general conferences, and I focused my thoughts and prayers in that direction. Although answers didn't come fast, I took courage from President James E. Faust, who said, "My reason for wanting to learn all I can about the Atonement is partly selfish: Our salvation depends on believing in and accepting the Atonement. Such acceptance requires a continual effort to understand it more fully" ("The Atonement: Our Greatest Hope," *Ensign,* Nov. 2001, 18).

Some time later when I was working at the police station, we handled an incident one day where a suspect holed up in a building and refused to come out. It was unknown whether he possessed any weapons. In such critical incidents, the department sets up what they call a critical incident command post. I'm no trained expert here, but this is what I know: there are three main branches in the command post. One team leads negotiations with the suspect, one team concentrates on field operations and basically consists of coordinated SWAT teams, and the third post coordinates these two and makes decisions. My job was to keep a running log of things that happened in the command post and document the time of day, decisions that were made, and who made them.

During this particular critical incident, the command post happened to be physically stationed within earshot of the negotiations unit. Throughout most of the day, and among the incidental noise as people came and went, I heard bits and pieces of the negotiations with the suspect.

There is a critical time frame for negotiations and SWAT teams. If negotiations last too long and manpower is not adequate, then SWAT teams lose their optimal performance edge, which is ultimately a safety threat. On the other hand, if negotiations are cut short prematurely by having a SWAT team move in too swiftly, then there is a risk of "pushing" the suspect to a breaking point, and maybe someone could get hurt. It's difficult to know when the line is crossed between the SWAT team's alertness and the subject's breaking point. It would be a very tough call to make. Hopefully an experienced officer knows the limits of his team and is patient. In this particular incident, the call was finally made, and the SWAT team went in. When the SWAT team broke in, they found that the suspect had taken his life, apparently only moments before. Throughout the long day, we'd had every reason to hope things would turn out well with no loss of life. We were wrong.

I drove home that night with the reality that I had heard the conversations of a young man only moments before he took his life. One minute a young man was breathing and had options, and then suddenly he had none. I was mentally exhausted that night, and I'm sure that had something to do with my reactions. I cannot adequately describe the sadness I felt. I cried and prayed all the way home. I pleaded for application of the Atonement to help me work through some grief and to not carry that burden home to my family.

A few days later, one of the detectives brought in an elderly man for questioning about some child abuse allegations. This interview was recorded and displayed on a TV monitor in a closet, tucked away from casual observers. Occasionally, to assist the detective or for training, a prosecutor or other detectives watched the interviews in progress, and such was the case on this occasion.

I had always been careful to purposely not watch the interviews. For one thing, it wouldn't be appropriate to "casually" watch them. Besides, they are quite lengthy and I had work to do, and often great spans of time passed with nothing occurring but relatively boring rhetoric. Then, too, I didn't want to expose myself to a lot of filth if it wasn't necessary, as I didn't want my sensibilities being numbed or hardened. I will always regret that on this occasion I briefly stopped to view the monitor. I had heard that this particular detective was very good at interviewing, and I hadn't seen him "at work," so I stopped to observe his skill.

Well, you can probably imagine what I heard, and I won't assault your sensibilities by repeating it. As luck would have it, I happened to hit *the* five crucial minutes of the interview. Suffice it to say that I held it together until quitting time at the end of the day, then once again I cried all the way home—and this was only a few days after the suicide incident. I knew I had called on the Atonement to find solace when my heart was hurting the first time, but here I was needing it again to heal my sorrows.

The reason I tell you all this is because somewhere I had gotten the idea that I needed to "save up" my faith in some kind of faith reservoir for that crucial moment when I was going to need to "part the Red Sea." At that point, I thought, I could call on the Lord in full confidence because I had so much saved-up faith to lay on the sacrificial altar. I tended to try to not bother the Lord with the little things because I supposed He might grow weary of my pleadings. I had "parted the Red Sea" and used up some of the faith on the command post incident a few days before, and I was very reluctant to use a substantial amount more to once again heal a heart that had heard and seen too much. That's when a thought came to me quite clearly—that the Atonement is infinite in more ways than one. It's not just *wide enough* to cover every type of affliction and trial and error. It is also *deep enough* to heal again and again and again and again—even the same affliction and even when the hurts are extremely close together. *(Smack forehead here.)*

President James E. Faust said this:

> Our Redeemer took upon Himself all the sins, pains, infirmities, and sicknesses of all who have ever lived and will ever live. No one has ever suffered in any degree what He did. He knows our mortal trials by firsthand experience. It is a bit like us trying to climb Mount Everest and only getting up the first few feet. But He has climbed all 29,000 feet to the top of the mountain. He suffered more than any other mortal could. . . .
>
> The basic source for the healing of the soul is the Atonement of Jesus Christ. This is true whether it be from the pain of a personal tragedy or a terrible national calamity. ("The Atonement: Our Greatest Hope," 19–20)

So I learned something new about the Atonement—new to me anyway. The Atonement will clean me up from the effects of life as often as is necessary, if I call upon it in humility and faith, even if I need it several times in one week or one day. And the faith needed to access the Atonement is like the widow's cruse of oil that Elisha promised would never run dry. The Atonement has not only breadth, but also depth.

And even though I learned a whole new aspect to the Atonement that I wouldn't trade for anything, I decided I should probably find a new job. And Ralph agreed.

CHAPTER 8

Telltale Signs

If thirty-seven women, of which I was one, lined up in some commercial kitchen and we all fixed the very same meal, with the very same recipes, and lined the meals up on a counter in random order, my children would still know which one I fixed. It would be the crisp one. Some would call it burned. I would call it "finally done." I have cooked meals for thirty years and still cannot tell you what to use rosemary for. She can just buck up and do the dishes for all I care.

Yessirree, I have left my mark on my children. They will never again smell burned chili sauce and think of anyone but me. They will never again eat peach cobbler without looking for the imprint of a stove top burner on the bottom of the pan. They will never again eat pot roast without smothering it in gravy or ketchup first. Somewhere the culture in their cultural heritage ended up scorched to the bottom of a pan.

There is no doubt that I left my mark. We all leave our mark.

Through the years, my children have left home at some point or another and then subsequently come back for visits. My home may be wonderfully clean before they come (I can always hope), and they may pack up all their belongings when they leave, but even if they are very careful, they leave a mark on my home. Their clothes may find their way out of my washer and back into their luggage and their bodies may go back to school or to their own homes, but an observer could still discern that they had been here—hairspray splotches on the bathroom mirror, wrinkled pillowcases, the bedspread slightly askew, the fridge and pantry *a lot* emptier, a dirty cup or dish in the TV room. And there will always be telltale clutter around the computer where they've kept up their email accounts and printed out tests and transcripts and study notes. I'm not complaining. *I'm just sayin'.* We all leave our mark. There are ways to tell when someone has been through your home—there are telltale signs.

People do the same thing to each other's lives. We leave telltale signs on each other, little imprints of our presence when passing through. Although it was many years ago now, I have little imprints of several Primary teachers: Sister Lillis Helsley, Sister Viola Williams, Sister Mae Marchello, and Sister Glenda May. They were wonderfully kind to me and I thought the world of them. As an adult, I now look back and think, "What a hodgepodge of women they were," because they each had problems that I can identify now as an adult that I didn't see as a child. I know I was their "assignment," but I wonder if somehow we were therapeutic for each other. I gave them an outlet for affection and helped them use their nurturing and homemaking talents, and they taught me skills, knew my name, and had a sweet smile, a hug, and a kind word for me each week. How grateful I am to them. They helped me achieve all of the little sequins for my green Primary bandalo and helped me pass off memorization of the Articles of Faith. I kept my little salt-dough and milk-carton recreation of Bethlehem for years. Sister Marchello even finished my crocheted rug when I finally held up my lopsided yarn mess and told her I couldn't do it anymore. She told me she thought I'd done enough to fulfill that requirement, which was a huge relief to me. I was afraid I couldn't be part of the Church anymore if I couldn't crochet. She saved me from the fiery, twisted hell of polyester yarn skeins.

Gene Gines also left her signature upon me. Gene was our neighbor. She had ten children of her own and drove a little Volkswagen bug. Every Primary day, we piled into the Volkswagen, sitting three or four deep on each others' laps, and drove home from Primary. Gene was so kind. She never yelled once that I recall. Not once. She never got frustrated, and Gene always knew my name—never called me by my sisters' names. She sent me notes in the mail when I gave a Sunday School talk or passed some other childhood milestone. She called me just the other day, in fact, to let me know she'd been thinking about me. She laughed about how old she looked but said she didn't feel old until she looked in the mirror. I shared my frustration that for the past five years, store clerks have been calling me "dear" and "honey," and I am clearly too young to be called "dear" by a total stranger. Gene's husband passed away a year ago, and she said she'd been busy attending the events of her grandchildren and great-grandchildren, including tending a great-grandchild so that the child's mother could finish a school term. I told her she was giving her children a great service by staying involved in their lives. She said, "Oh, I hadn't thought of it that way. I just can't bear the thought of missing out." At the close of our conversation, Gene told me she was proud of me and that she loved me. It made me tear up; I hadn't heard that from a motherly figure in a very long time, maybe even since Primary days. Yes, Gene has left her mark on me. There are telltale signs.

We all leave our little telltale signs on the people who pass through our lives. So the next time you have a chance to make an impact, make it a good one. Make it a great one. I'm just sayin'.

CHAPTER 9

Endearing Humanity

I try so hard to be perfect . . . and then I lose my slip.

It was my mother-in-law's eightieth birthday party. The family wanted to have a really nice celebration event for her. A *nice* event in my book would have included jeans, flip-flops, Popsicles, and water guns. But a nice event for my mother-in-law is not even addressed in the same lobes of the brain or in the same global hemispheres. Her children planned a very nice dinner at the Joseph Smith Memorial Building in Salt Lake City, with a photographer to take pictures by the reflecting pool. Now who can't appreciate that? I'll tell you who—*someone without a slip.* I knew there was something I had forgotten to pack. And you just can't wear a filmy skirt, even if it's lined, on a sunny day when there's a breeze without a slip, people. Even jeans and flip-flop gals know this.

So, I'm in the hotel room trying to figure out how I can keep my thighs clenched and walk two blocks to the dinner. I look around, and there beside me on the air conditioner are my son's shorts. They're the "I-can't-believe-they-put-that-much-material-into-a-pair-of-shorts," khaki, fifty-saddlebag-pockets-on-the-thighs kind. It's true that my son Levi had worn them to float the river in Jackson Hole the day before, so they were a little stiff and scratchy, but we're talking eightieth birthday party here. SO . . . . I put those babies on right under my filmy skirt and there was enough saddlebag billow to fill it out and more. My skirt was a little lumpy, but there was no blue sky between my thighs, and that was the goal. I was a dadgum genius!

Now in about thirty years when I look back at the pictures of my mother-in-law's eightieth birthday party, I'm probably not going to remember the white cake with cream and fruit filling covered with fondant, or the pretty pearl and diamond stick pin that the family gave her, or all the kind words that were spoken. But I'd bet ten to one that I still remember wearing scratchy, billowing saddlebag shorts under my dress. And I'll still probably have a good laugh over it then. At least I didn't have to worry about someone saying, "Honey, your slip is showing."

Now, be honest. Who hasn't got a similar story? We sisters in the gospel work so hard at trying to be heavenly perfect, but every single day we're reminded of how human we are. It's actually sometimes our humanity that is so endearing. Our humanity binds us—even if it's a trauma bond.

I love those things that bind us.

I love that we cannot balance our church bags while wearing four-inch heels, so we wear flat, rubber-soled shoes because we're in that three-hour meeting block for the long haul.

I love that we get choked up when someone else's son is preparing for his mission.

I love that we have a "widows' row" in Relief Society (not because they're all widows, but because they come with or without husbands, with or without support; they just come).

I love that we cannot put the right context to "Four score and seven years ago . . ." but we can remember all three verses of "Give Said the Little Stream." Except for that part about whether it's the grass or the fields growing greener.

I love that the old-timers still sing "You who unto Jesus" during "How Firm a Foundation."

I love that we miss the original tune to "Know This That Every Soul Is Free."

I love that we're so nervous when teaching a lesson we overcompensate with table toppers, pictures of family, and decorations.

I love that we smile when, like clockwork, the same two or three people approach the podium to bear testimonies each and every testimony meeting.

I love that Primary opening exercises never go the way we think they will.

I love that we decoupage, scrapbook, and jump on the bandwagon of every new craft in Relief Society.

I love it that we approach visitors to introduce ourselves and find out these people have been members of our wards for a good three weeks now.

I love that we quilt and chat.

I love that when we leave our cereal at home, someone in the next pew shares hers.

I love that we forfeit our favorite pew when we see that someone's family is visiting and needs the room.

I love that we dress babies in white for blessings and try so very hard to remember the words of the blessing to record in our journals.

I love that we smile at each other even if we haven't learned one another's names.

I love that we have little notes written in the margins of our scriptures.

I love it that we become best friends when working in a presidency together.

I love it that three years or so after being released from a presidency, we lose touch a little but can pick up the friendship right where we left off at any given point in time.

I love that when we have missionaries leaving, our friends drop by with salads or rolls or casseroles to help feed the family who is bravely pretending not to be in mourning.

I love that when someone in my family is truly ill, the food comes flooding in like a rainforest downpour, even though there's not a chance in the world we'll starve to death.

I love it that when someone we're close to passes away, even the sisters who didn't know the individual will fill the mailbox with sympathy cards.

I love it that we attend funerals for people we didn't know just to lend support to the mourners.

I love it that we carry surprises in our scripture bags to keep children entertained during sacrament meeting, even if the children are not ours.

I love it that our choirs try hard.

I love that our stomachs growl so loudly on fast Sunday.

I love it that our prayers are unrehearsed.

We celebrate birthdays and anniversaries, retirements and promotions, but we don't celebrate our humanity. I'm not saying we should relish the natural man. I'm just saying that humanity strips us of our vanity, and we should celebrate that.

CHAPTER 10

Living Water

I grew up in southern Idaho on a farm watered by an irrigation tract fed by the Salmon River and collected in a reservoir. Sufficient water for our agricultural needs was always a worry. If our local snow packs weren't heavy enough, the crops would not produce, and bills would not be paid. So every year (at least it seemed like every year) we prayed in family prayer that we would receive sufficient water for the crops. Not just once a year, mind you, but from November to May we prayed for water. I got sick of praying for water. Our little community congregation also held fasts for water. I got sick of fasting for water.

Our farm was lucky—it had two additional small reservoirs that were filled by Deep Creek (a sad misnomer). But many years Deep Creek barely ran at all because the hills held no snow. Nonetheless, we had more water than other farms.

Lastly, to boost the water resources on our farm, my father decided to drill an irrigation well. It was an expensive risk, and he gave my mother hourly updates on the drilling—how deep they were, whether they were seeing any signs of progress, whether the casing would hold. This required another round of fervent prayers for water—always water. Water, or the lack thereof, came to dominate our community, and I got really tired of hearing about it.

Another reminder of how pervasive the water concern was came when I told my grandfather I wanted to help him write his life story. Grandpa wasn't very talkative, but Grandma said it wouldn't be a problem because Grandpa had faithfully written diaries for years. I was excited by that and thought this would assist the process tremendously. Grandma went to the back bedroom and brought out several shoeboxes that held small diaries—mostly the lock and key kind. I eagerly began searching the entries but quickly found that each day's entry listed the weather conditions, the growth or harvest state of the crops, sometimes a crop price, and a record of how much water was running in Deep Creek or the water level in the dams. That was it. I began looking up special days, like the birth of a daughter, to see if there wasn't something more written. But nope—just the weather, a crop report, and the water situation.

I felt so lucky when we finally moved off the Salmon Tract and found a home twelve miles north on the Snake River floodplain where there was much more water available. Instead of hay bales being spaced so infrequently as on the Salmon Tract, the Snake River plain had hay fields with twice the tonnage. I wondered if the people there knew how lucky they were. Apparently they didn't. I sat in church one early winter day and was stunned when the brother conducting the meeting asked everyone to pray AND FAST for more water. I had very irreverent thoughts like, "You have got to be kidding me! Don't you get it? You HAVE water. You have no idea just how much water you have!" It seemed almost sacrilege to have a community so blessed with water fasting and praying for more. It seemed greedy.

That was about fifteen years ago. Over the next fifteen years, I bet we've been asked to pray and fast for water during thirteen of them. Thirteen. I hit a breaking point in Sunday School class one day when the subject was brought up. I said, "Maybe we ought to quit fasting and praying for more water and realize we live in a desert. Maybe we ought to pray for the wisdom to use wisely what we have and cultivate less ground. Remember, THIS IS A DESERT."

It didn't go over too well. I was quickly bombarded with instructions to increase my faith. I was reminded that the Lord had promised the desert would "blossom as the rose." I was familiar with that promise. I just happened to think the Lord meant for us to blossom like a cactus rose, not a rainforest rose—but I could be wrong. I'm still confused by the response it evoked. What was not hard to figure out was that our community economy depended on water and it didn't matter if you were a farmer, an economist, a dentist, or a construction worker. If there wasn't enough snow, we were in trouble. Mortgages would go unpaid.

Water—always water. I was tired of praying for water. Most of the time, I admit, I gave the prayers and fasts only minimal effort.

Last year I visited a woman in Indiana for a weekend. She was immensely proud of her yard (and with good reason) and wanted to show me her efforts—her garden, herbs, flowers, and bushes. So I walked with her through her yard, warily looking out for any sprinkler heads lest I should trip, as she told me the names of her plants. After several minutes I realized there were no sprinkler heads, hence no underground sprinkling system. I was surprised. It was an upscale neighborhood and surely one would reasonably expect an underground sprinkling system. Furthermore, I could see no hoses being dragged around. Upon further inspection I realized THERE WERE NO OUTDOOR WATER FAUCETS on the house. How then, I wondered, could such a beautiful landscape be watered? So, I asked this sister, "How do you water your lawn?" She looked at me rather quizzically and said, "That's the rain's job."

I was stunned. When I couldn't immediately grasp that concept to respond quickly enough, she apologetically continued. "But the lawn isn't in great shape because we've had sort of a drought. It's been *ten days* since the last rain."

Ten days. Clearly, this gal had no clue what a drought was. Where could I even begin to correct her misconception? I'll bet she had never fasted or prayed for water in her life. Lucky gal.

As we later drove to the airport, we passed fields of corn and other crops I couldn't identify, and I couldn't see any pivots or wheel lines in the fields. I puzzled over this for some time before

I found the courage to ask how farmers watered their crops. My host looked at me like maybe I was a little slow and simply repeated, "That's the rain's job." Unbelievable. I thought back again of the many fasts and prayers from my community asking for water. A significant part of my life was spent fasting and praying for something this woman would never understand the value of.

Jesus knew about water and thirst when He, "being wearied with his journey," asked the Samaritan woman at the well for a drink and she questioned Him why He would ask her, a Samaritan, for a drink when "Jews have no dealings with the Samaritans. Jesus answered and said unto her, If thou knewest the gift of God, and who it is that saith to thee, Give me to drink; thou wouldest have asked of him, and he would have given thee living water. The woman saith unto him, Sir, thou hast nothing to draw with, and the well is deep: from whence then hast thou that living water? . . . Jesus answered and said unto her, Whosoever drinketh of this water shall thirst again: But whosoever drinketh of the water that I shall give him shall never thirst; but the water that I shall give him shall be in him a well of water springing up into everlasting life" (John 4:6–14).

Why do I tell you all this? A temple was recently built within ten miles of my home. Ten miles! For Saints in our community there will be no more trips over icy, snow-packed roads to attend a temple two hours away. No more budgeting for the gas to get there and the babysitter to take care of the kids until we return. No more napping through the temple sessions because we had to drive all the way there and will have to drive yet all the way home. No more packing sandwiches for the trip. No more arranging buses and carpools. I know these were small sacrifices to make and having a temple even two hours away was a tremendous blessing. But now with a temple in our midst, it feels like Indiana has come to the Salmon Tract, as we have the opportunity now to partake so freely of the living water made available through the temple. It's so close. Receiving the peace, the power, and the ordinances is so thirst quenching. It's indescribably sweet.

There will always be valleys more fertile than those in southern Idaho, and as sure as I live in a desert, I'm sure I will be asked yet again to fast for water in years ahead. But I will now fast and pray with more sincerity because this I know: those years of our community fasting and praying for "living waters" were worth it after all. Our prayers were heard in a way few of us had anticipated.

CHAPTER 11

Fly on the Wall

When my sons went on missions, I thought I would feel really noble. Instead, I felt really lonely. I felt grateful, too, and lucky. But mostly lonely. I just wanted to be a fly on the wall for five minutes and see my boys settled in their new surroundings. If it had been appropriate, I totally would have flown to South Dakota and Alabama, sat in a car across the street, and watched my sons come and go from their apartments. That's all I needed. Just a glimpse.

Well, sisters, be careful what you wish for. My own sons are home from their missions, and now I'm finally the fly on the wall since we became a missionary host family.

"Elder, what *is* that smell? You're not boiling socks, are you?" Unfortunately, I'm the fly with an above-average sense of smell.

"Soup."

"For *breakfast?*"

"It's good for you. And it makes a whole lot." Judging by the size of his pot, I'd say he's right about the last part.

"No soup I ever made smelled like that. What's in it?"

"Are you sure you want to know?" He's right. I don't.

"Just turn on the kitchen fan and light the candle." I make a mental note that my scented candles aren't lasting as long since the full-time elders moved into our basement. I can't resist peeking into the pot when he leaves the room. Noodles. Cabbage. Spam. Who buys Spam? Wasn't that a World War II food? I didn't know they still made it. Onions. Eggs. Other unrecognizable floaties. All good things, in theory, but it's not even seven o'clock in the morning yet. *What is he thinking?* That is, of course, a rhetorical question because it has become abundantly apparent that I will never be able to figure out what the thought process of an elder is.

New day, different scenario involving . . . *dun, dun, dun* . . . the refrigerator. "Elder, you're not going to eat that."

"Why not?"

"Have you seen the expiration date on that sliced ham?"

"There's an expiration date?"

"I can smell it from here. Trust me, there's an expiration date. Find my glasses and I'll prove it to you." How did he manage to live this long without being salmonelled, botulismed, or molded to death? I'll bet he swallowed his gum when he was a kid, too. "And you might as well throw out the rest of the food down there on the bottom shelf. It's been there for two transfers. I don't think it's getting any younger."

Then one evening one of the elders asked me if we had an extra bike. I was a little puzzled because they drive a car everywhere, but I assumed it was none of my business.

"Sure. I think there's a couple extra in the garage. You might have to pump up a tire or two."

"So what time do you think we should leave to get to Jackpot?"

"Jackpot? You mean Jackpot, Nevada?"

"Yeah."

I knew he was from California and was perhaps geographically challenged, but was he serious? "This is southern IDAHO. Nevada is fifty miles from here, even if it is still in your mission. It's uphill. It's January. Are you kidding me?"

"We can do it." It was awfully generous to offer this feat for his companion, as well, who couldn't have weighed one hundred thirty pounds soaking wet. "I'm a cross-country runner."

"You WERE a cross-country runner, Elder—WERE. You've been out of shape now for about four months." He clearly wasn't fazed.

"Wait." I was trying hard not to laugh out loud. "Hold that thought. I want Fred to hear this."

I dragged Fred into the room. "Okay, Elder, tell Fred what you told me." And he did. And Fred thought it was as funny as I did.

"So you think it's too cold?"

"You bet your sweet bippy it is."

So they argued back and forth for a bit, the elder insisting he could do it and Fred trying to explain how crazy he was. Finally, I figured out how to end it.

"Elder, this is not about how strong you are or how willing you are to endure the elements to teach an investigator. Sacrifice is one thing, but the Lord does not compensate us for stupidity. This is about health and safety and life. It's January. Idaho winters are brutal, and the current weather inversion means the fog reduces visibility to maybe a hundred yards on a dangerous stretch of highway. You are not riding bikes to Nevada in the fog. You. Will. Die. End of discussion." I don't think he was very grateful for my input. Thank heavens they had to ask for a second bike or I have no doubt they'd have taken off without consulting us. In short, I refused to lend the bike and they had to hitch a ride with members.

Now missionary moms, don't you worry. Your sons are fine. Really. They're not real bright yet in some ways (which you already knew), but they're doing fine. From my fly-on-the-wall position this morning, I heard one elder say the blessing over his breakfast (which, undoubtedly, has kept him salmonella-free so far), and among other things, he sought blessings for his family . . . right after he prayed to stay awake during the Sunday meetings. I know for a fact the Lord is protecting him because you're praying for him, and you and I both know the Lord cannot leave a young man like that on his own.

CHAPTER 12

No Charity for the Referee

If charity will get me into heaven, then I want you to know I have the "suffereth long" part down pretty well because that's exactly what I do at high school basketball games with lousy refereeing.

"Did you not see that?" I say to the empty bleacher beside me. "How could that referee not see that?"

Then all in one breath I am not kind, I seeketh my own, I am easily provoked, and I thinketh evil. "Oh my gosh, that was a horrible call. He anticipated that foul but it never happened. All ball. You're killing me, ref. You're just killing me." I say this to the back of the head sitting in front of me and roll my eyes.

I've watched the local crowds at our home games, and especially the Latter-day Saints. If I'm having trouble with charity, then I darn well know I'm not alone. Yes, I know, some of our brethren and sisters are sitting demurely and look almost comatose. I cannot explain this. Do they not envieth the other team's eight fouls to our twenty-five? Do they hopeth that things will get better, that the other team won't cutteth the knees out from under the post player? I just hopeth there is no blood by the end of the game, but I believeth there is a good chance of this. Then the mouthy fan behind me (there's always one who cannot mumbleth his opinions to himself) yells at the offending player, "Good job, Bubba. Way to give it to 'em." And it is too much. I puffeth up. I let 'er rippeth (but only in my mind), "How can you call yourself a human? You're disgusting. You're nauseating. Put a cork in it! Who let you into the gym? No one wants to hear your opinion—get that through your head." And charity simply flyeth out the window. You know it's true.

I asked one of my sons how he suggested someone handle this situation. His reply was, "When I went to the game, I had someone sit by me who said everything for me." Then he admitted that thinking the insults in our heads without blurting them out is probably only slightly redeeming.

I've heard it said there is no competition in the celestial kingdom, which might solve my little dilemma. My son Homer takes issue with this, however. In his words, "I would like to see the doctrine for no competition in the celestial kingdom. I believe this is only rumor, because I just can't see Jesus and Peter, James, John, Grandpa, and many others sitting around saying, 'Boy I hope we win the battle with Satan, but if not, it's okay, as long as we try our best and have fun.' I just don't see that happening!" He has a point.

I'm actually hoping he's right, that maybe a little competition does creep in. Otherwise, I'm afraid only the comatose will be there. (We're all thinking it. I'm just the one who said it.)

CHAPTER 13

Healthy

So I went to a physician's assistant the other day for a sinus infection. I made the appointment for right after lunch hour so I wouldn't have to wait—at least wait long. A lady pulled up beside me in the parking lot. Yessirree, I was going to have to beat her to the door so my name got on the patient roster first. I booked it.

Later, as I sat in my little tissue-paper covering (because we might as well do the annual exam, right?), the physician's assistant wasted no chit-chat but straightforwardly asked if I had a healthy diet. Of course. As a member of the Church, I don't smoke, drink, do illegal drugs, abuse prescription drugs, or eat fast food very often (never, if it isn't on the dollar menu). That makes me basically a health nut. I smugly thought of the promise, "they that wait upon the Lord shall renew their strength; they shall mount up with wings as eagles; they shall run, and not be weary; and they shall walk, and not faint" (Isaiah 40:31). You betcha, Doctor, bring it on.

"Oh," she said, "so you get five servings of fruits and vegetables?"

"Um, well, only three, errr—maybe two." She jotted this on her pad.

"So you drink milk?"

"Well, maybe once every two weeks" (and only if it's completely drowning in Nestlé Nesquik, but I spared her the details). More jotting.

"You get a few servings of cheese, then?"

"Not exactly."

"Yogurt?"

Okay, I'm sorry, but that stuff looks gross. "You know it's curdled milk, don't you?" And if she had grown up on a farm, she'd have known that we used to feed it to our weiner pigs as whey. At any rate, she had no idea that I had something better than yogurt—I had obedience on my side and shall "receive health in [my] navel and marrow to [my] bones."

"Orange juice?"

"Nnnnnoooooo." Couldn't she appreciate the fact that it's Girl Scout cookie season and I only bought four boxes instead of six?

"Soy milk?"

I laughed. No farm girl ever drank soy milk. That's for . . . for . . . hmmmm, I wonder how it tastes with Nesquik. *Jot, jot, jot.*

"Well, if you're not getting vegetables, fruit, calcium, vitamin C, or basically any other vitamins, then you're taking a multivitamin, right?"

Now hold on a minute. Let's get this clear, sweetheart, you are not my bishop or my stake president, and this is not a recommend interview, so just lighten up.

I countered weakly, "I read somewhere those aren't FDA approved." She was not impressed. And to think I beat the lady in the parking lot to get in here.

"How about exercise?"

"Well, see, I have this hip pain. It's listed right there on one of the fifteen forms you had me fill out. You know I came in for a sinus infection, right?"

"Have you tried anything for it?"

"The sinuses?"

"The hip pain."

"Like what?"

"Ibuprofen, glucosamine?"

"That's for old people." Jotting again.

"When was your last mammogram?" Now that's a little personal, don't you think?

"Colonoscopy?"

I had to chuckle. I did not want to have that discussion today. "You mean having one? Don't they, uh . . . you know. I mean . . . you're not going to make me say it, are you?" She wasn't the least bit sympathetic. And someone needed to tell her to wear a little mascara. "I'll think about it. Let me get back to you."

She needed to know that my promise is to "run and not be weary, walk and not faint." But somehow I was feeling sicker by the minute.

An hour later, I left her office with a Band-Aid over a hole in the crook of my right arm, a calcium education list, and six brand-spankin' new prescriptions. Six. I felt like my mother— who was always very old, by the way—and I still had a sinus infection. Next time I'm going to bring my Doctrine and Covenants with me and let her write the prescription in Section 89.

CHAPTER 14

The unwritten rule is if your husband is a banker, you don't bother him with your deposits and withdrawals. If your husband is a plumber, you put Roto-Rooter on speed dial. If your husband is a farmer, don't expect help in the garden. The rule is universal. We know it; we respect it.

For the same unspoken reasons, I do not tell people I meet that I am an author. People tend to assume that if I sometimes write, then I love to write. I don't. It's very hard. *Painful* is a better word. Please-rap-my-knuckles-with-a-ruler-and-make-me-bleed-instead is even more apropos. I tend to make sure my laundry is done first, the mending, the ironing, the food trap in the dishwasher cleaned, the Easter decoration box organized, the books in the bookcase alphabetized (not that any of those things are done, mind you).

Another reason I don't volunteer information about my writing life is that I have so much improvement to make that it feels hypocritical to offer writing advice, and people tend to want writing advice. You'd be surprised at the number of people who want a little writing advice. Like I have any. I'm a student myself.

And the last reason I don't tell people I write is that people tend to think that writers are also editors. Of course we're editors. No one is more critical of our own writing than we are. But I can't turn off that critical eye just because the writing isn't my own. It's shred and shred-alike. Some people want me to read what they've written and give them advice. Hard experience has taught me that most people don't really want critique;

they want praise. None of us likes to be told our manuscript needs a lot of work and revising. We don't want to hear that our toddling creations, born inside our little brains, need a kick in the pants and a fresh approach—a diaper change, as it were. And I simply have no tactful way of telling someone that their writing needs a lot of work. I need—and the rest of the writing world needs—the brutal teacher or editor. I just don't want to *be* that editor. So I became a liar.

One young elder who was living in our basement said, "Sister Jaynes, do you want to read the poem I've been writing?"

"No. Under no circumstances do I want to read your poem. I will murder it, and by extension you, and we need to be on speaking terms so I can tell you when to clean the bathroom," is what I *should* have said. Instead I really said, "Sure. What's it about?" And then I kicked myself and contemplated boiling myself in oil or searing my eyes with a hot poker.

"It's about a guitar-man wizard." Did I hear that correctly?

"A *who?*"

"Guitar-man wizard." Somebody just shoot me now. "You're kidding, right?"

Nope, he wasn't. "This guitar-man wizard, does he save the world or a maiden in distress or protect the world from evil? Because I'm really not visualizing this. Does he ride on his guitar to save someone? Does he use his pick or neck strap to out-whip someone? Out-poke someone? What are his assets?"

"He's magic."

Well, of course he is. That says it all, doesn't it? That's what happens when kids grow up with tales of magic kingdoms and heros with magic powers instead of tales of good ol' cowboys and Indians.

I thought of so many things to say to this young man— things like, "You won't quit your day job just yet, will you?" or "You *are* going to get a college degree, right?" How was I going to be positive about this? I didn't have to read it. If I said it was brilliant, I knew I'd be lying. *Guitar-man?* Come on. Nobody's going to buy that.

"I just wrote it for fun." Great. Then I will crush your fun. I would rather chew my freckles off. Maybe he would forget about it? But he left it for me on the table. I couldn't bear to read it in front of him. I picked it up and said, "I'll read it before I go to bed tonight." That would give me a whole night to craft an answer.

Next morning, bless my heart, I was as positive as I knew how to be. "Well, that *was* fun. That's quite an imagination you've got." And no question, it was imaginative. "I don't know that I'm buying into guitar-man . . . that kinda blows my mind a little . . . but it's certainly imaginative." Notice I hadn't lied yet? Trust me, I was planning to. But my daughter Rachel saved me. She picked it up and started reading and giggled all the way through it. I think the young man was very pleased with her response. Bada-bing, bada-boom! Why hadn't I thought of that before? Put a cute girl to reading his creation and all is right with his world. Brilliant. Absolutely brilliant. Wish I'd thought of it. Wish I'd had the tact to handle the whole thing better right from the get-go.

Tact is not my forte. Ergo the lack of light, casual conversation with friends, like the guy who commented on my haircut. "Men like long hair, you know." I couldn't believe a male acquaintance was actually saying that to me after I just chopped off my hair. Who made him spokesman for the whole man-world? I thought of a long string of nasty remarks, but in the end I tried not to lash back too severely.

"Frankly, I care less and less about that every year." I'm not sure he even got my point. Doesn't matter because *he started it.* (What am I? Seven years old?)

Other than that one remark, I tried to take comments about my haircut from others more lightly. "This is my midlife crisis— I was always a late bloomer. I just couldn't afford a Corvette." Granted, the haircut is very short. Very. And yes, I painted the kitchen green about the same time, but c'mon—a midlife crisis? That would imply I only had one crisis per lifetime. If we base definition of a midlife crisis on a drastic hair change, then I've had a plethora. And I'm planning several more. Man-world, beware (and then grow up for crying out loud because I fear my tact-ship has sailed).

I just like a little change once in a while. Haircut? Green paint? Who doesn't like a little change? Oh wait—tactfully put, that would be Fred.

"Do you want to go to a movie tonight?" This would be a real change from our regular Friday please-don't-drag-me-out-of-the-house fare.

"No."

"But *will* you go to a movie tonight with me?" This, of course, creates a dilemma for him. If he says yes, he'll hate it. He only wants to relax in his easy chair after a long week of work. He wants a nice, quiet supper. He doesn't even want conversation. If he says no, then it implies that he won't sacrifice a little for me, his wife, and our relationship. He knows he'll pay for that. Such a dilemma. What will he do?

"Well, I don't really want to, but I guess I could." Smart move. He's trying to make me *feel his pain.* That way, if I insist on going, then it would be my fault the relationship suffers because I'm pressing him to do something he doesn't want to do and might even be detrimental to his rest. But if I acquiesce, then let's face it—I will never see a movie. I will be relegated to every Adam Sandler rerun on the movie channel. Now *that's* pain. But now the ball is in my court, so to speak. Shall I bring out the arsenal? Remind him that he's not going to my nephew's or niece's weddings, didn't go to see my Washington and Alaska siblings conveniently visiting in Utah, didn't go to the last family reunion, refuses to go camping with me and the grand-kids, and we just spent Memorial Day with *his family?* The real question here is, do I want to use up that arsenal on this battle or save it for later when I really need to sink his sub—which might be the day I drive home a Corvette? What will I do?

"Not a problem, hon. I don't mind going alone." (Believe me—been there, done that. But it doesn't change the fact that it was a lie.) "But I think I'll treat myself to supper, too, so you'll have to find some leftovers." (He hates that. And whether he admits it or not, he really doesn't like me being gone, either. It's apparently no fun having the TV remote if there isn't someone there to *keep it from,* and even he gets bored with the Adam Sandler reruns.)

So midlife crises are good for something after all. It enabled me to finally handle an irritating conversation with tact. Yes, I think I now have tact—ulterior-motive tact, maybe, but I'll take what I can get. I tell myself it counts (and that's only a *white* lie).

CHAPTER 15

I Had It All Wrong

I had it all wrong. Some twenty years ago, my son Homer, when he was in second grade, gifted me a handmade Christmas tree ornament. It was a glass ball covered with what was probably paint, although it's hard to pinpoint just exactly what the glop is. It resembles nasal discharge, green phlegm, green pus—all three, and in several bacterial colors. I fondly call it the ugliest Christmas ornament ever. He managed to glue a sprig of plastic holly to the top, either that or the teacher took it upon herself to hide the worst of it. She failed. I mean truly, this is the ugliest little ornament ever. That's why I love it. And that's why I was so surprised the other day when Homer came by my office to show me his latest work of art. He's picked up the hobby of metal art and had made a campfire ring to show me. And it was pretty dang good. I sure didn't see that one coming. How in the world did he get from a ball of green pus to pine trees and ducks, cattails and sunflowers? I don't get it.

Then there's my youngest daughter, Rachel. Rachel is one of the happiest and most fun people I know, but we don't take her to restaurants if we can possibly avoid it. There are just too many choices on the menu, and she cannot make up her mind. Finally, on one family trip, Fred quit asking her what she wanted to order. He'd count to about ten, and if she hadn't ordered, then he ordered for her. She had to eat whatever he chose. We thought that would cure her. It didn't. It just made her mad. Also, clothes shopping with her is not an option. She wrestles and wrestles with her indecisions and wears us out. I speak for all of us. However, she graduated with her bachelor's

degree an entire semester early (which is a very big deal to
parents), and why? Because she has known since her freshman
year what she wanted to do and she never wavered. Not once.
Not when her aunt tried to talk her out of it. Not when she
knew she'd have to get a graduate degree for it to be useful. I
encouraged her to take a few fun classes along the way, enjoy
the journey, but nope, she knew what she wanted, and she
knew how to get it. Good for her. I never would have thought
Rachel could make up her mind that quickly and firmly. I was
completely blindsided by that one.

And then there's Levi, my fourth child. Levi has been one of
the most content children I have known. He doesn't withdraw
from adventure, but he hasn't necessarily sought it out, either.
He's just content, always has been. But he just called me from
Virginia, where he and his wife will set up house and he will
teach school. Virginia. Do you know how far away from Idaho
that is? What the daisies did he go to Virginia for? Apparently
he was less content than I thought. The good news is they have
so much to offer. They have testimonies and educations and will
be able to start their family and forge into the job force during
a stressed economy absolutely debt free. How many people can
say that?

I just misjudged them all. Didn't know them as well
as I thought I did. Apparently, I couldn't tell diddly from
squat. That's what's so darned frustrating about mortality, eh?
Unpredictable. That's what's *so great* about mortality though,
isn't it? The surprise? The unexpected blessings? I just have to
learn not to trip over the blessings.

About the Author

Lynn C. Jaynes was born in southern Idaho, was raised in southern Idaho, and has raised her five children in southern Idaho with her husband, Fred. She's eaten a lot of potatoes. Those are the only things about her life that do not change. The rest is always in flux.

She explains, "I just want you all to know straight out that I am not related to any Youngs, Smiths, Kimballs, Monsons, Bensons, Packers, or Hinckleys. I do not have any direct ancestors who were mission presidents or stake presidents (that I know of). I do not have even thirdhand experiences or conversations with General Authorities to relate. I did not have an ancestor who pulled a handcart, got frostbite, or was buried on the plains. I do, however, come from a long line of Primary, Sunday School, seminary, and Young Women teachers, people who baked bread and fixed funeral potatoes and tried to remember whether or not Captain Moroni was the same Moroni who abridged the golden plates. I come from people with mostly good hearts. And that's okay."